HOARD

Fleur Adcock was born in New Zealand in 1934. She spent the war years in England, returning with her family to New Zealand in 1947. She emigrated to Britain in 1963, working as a librarian in London until 1979. In 1977-78 she was writer-in-residence at Charlotte Mason College of Education, Ambleside. She was Northern Arts Literary Fellow in 1979-81, living in Newcastle, becoming a freelance writer after her return to London. She received an OBE in 1996, and the Queen's Gold Medal for Poetry in 2006 for *Poems 1960-2000* (Bloodaxe Books, 2000).

Fleur Adcock published three pamphlets with Bloodaxe: *Below Loughrigg* (1979), *Hotspur* (1986) and *Meeting the Comet* (1988), as well as her translations of medieval Latin lyrics, *The Virgin & the Nightingale* (1983). All her other collections were published by Oxford University Press until they shut down their poetry list in 1999, after which Bloodaxe published her collected poems, *Poems 1960-2000* (2000), followed by *Dragon Talk* (2010), *Glass Wings* (2013), *The Land Ballot* (2015) and *Hoard* (2017). *Poems 1960-2000* is a Poetry Book Society Special Commendation and *Glass Wings* a Poetry Book Society Recommendation.

FLEUR ADCOCK

Hoard

BLOODAXE BOOKS

First published 2017 by
Bloodaxe Books Ltd,
Eastburn,
South Park,
Hexham,
Northumberland NE46 1BS.

www.bloodaxebooks.com
For further information about Bloodaxe titles
please visit our website or write to
the above address for a catalogue.

Supported using public funding by
ARTS COUNCIL
ENGLAND

Cover design: Neil Astley & Pamela Robertson-Pearce.

Printed in Great Britain by Bell & Bain Limited, Glasgow, Scotland, on
acid-free paper sourced from mills with FSC chain of custody certification.

For my granddaughters
– Lily, Julia, Cait, Ella, Rosa –
and my grandson Ollie.

ACKNOWLEDGEMENTS

Acknowledgements are due to the editors of the following publications in which some of these poems first appeared: *broadsheet/19*, *Hwaet: 20 Years of Ledbury Poetry Festival*, *Katherine Mansfield Studies*, *Ploughshares*, *New Zealand Books*, *PN Review*, *Poetry London*, *Poetry Review*, *The Rialto*, *The Spectator*, *The Spinoff* (New Zealand), *The Times Literary Supplement*, the *University of Reading Creative Arts Anthology 2017* and *The Yellow Nib*.

'Albatross' and 'The March' were commissioned by the Bristol Festival of Ideas in 2015 and 2016 respectively.

CONTENTS

I

Loot

'A COVENTRY HALFE PENNY': a token
minted in 1669
by some trader in that city
to make up for a shortage of small change

and sucked in the mouth of history
for so long that its outer edges
are smoothed away, gone down time's gullet
with a slow wince of dissolving copper.

Fondling it in my early teens,
and too bedazzled by its date to be
logical about geography,
I used to see it in the hand of Pepys.

But then, why shouldn't it have travelled?
After all, it found its way to me.
It could have jingled in the same pocket
as this, from the official coinage:

a hefty farthing, 1675,
half the face value but twice the volume,
with the rugged mug of the second Charles,
'Carolus a Carolo', crowned in laurel.

It could even have met my silver groat –
William and Mary, 1691,
with their unfortunate Stuart profiles
and a hole punched through the top of his wreath.

*

These were gems from a clanking bag
our former evacuee brought me
(looted by her brother from a bombed house)
to make my collection thrice glorious:

worn, a lot of them, or defaced
(that watch-chain puncture); not valuable,
I know now, but I was a-goggle
at their ages. I spread them on the floor

to wallow in: farthings from ten reigns,
cartwheel pennies, every shade of metal
from Europe, strange brass from the East,
and a denarius of Constantine.

I sorted them, listed them, researched them,
and, my subconscious having been misled
into expecting sudden marvels,
dreamed them: I'd be floating along

some hazy beach or a simulacrum
of my local streets and see by my feet
one delicious coin after another,
in archaic, unheard of currencies,

lying there, anyone's for the taking.
Grab them, quick! Stuff them under the pillow;
and this time, if you really concentrate,
they'll still be there when you wake up.

Mnemonic

Nothing I write will be as durable
as the rhyme for remembering the genders
of third declension nouns, stuck in my head
ever since Miss Garai's Latin class.

Masculini generis

I used to fancy I shared it with
generations of English schoolboys,
the colonial servant dispensing justice
under a tree in the African bush,

are the nouns that end in -nis

the wakeful subaltern in the trenches
before the Somme; but now I discover
the rhyme was originally German,
as was Miss Garai. The vision shifts:

and mensis, sanguis, orbis, fons,

the solar topeed official sits
not in Nigeria, but in Kamerun;
the soldier is on the other side of
what looks very much like the same barbed wire,

collis, lapis, piscis, mons,

writing to his girlfriend. I'll call him Kurt,
like the pen-friend Miss Garai found for me
in the Germany she had escaped from
before another world war came round.

sermo, ordo, sol and pons,
dens, sal, as, grex, pulvis.

Her Usual Hand

My signature begins with a shape
I never use elsewhere: a relic
of the initial 'F' I was taught
in 'real writing' at my seventh school.

My writing became, if anything,
less real as further schools numbed it,
and the sprinting pace of lecture notes
crushed it into a kind of shorthand.

In my first library job, my boss
thrust a manual on penmanship
at me: the overdue cards I sent
brought shame on the University.

For all the charms of the special nib
and its trellis patterns on the page,
italic script was not the answer:
it was not writing; it was drawing.

So my friends couldn't read my letters?
Very well, I would learn to type them.
My private messages to myself
could remain in their workaday rags.

If handwriting mirrors character
all I can see mine reflecting is
my headlong scramble for the exit,
shouting something over my shoulder.

Six Typewriters

To begin with, my father's reconditioned
German keyboard picked up during the war,
with a spiky Gothic 'o'.
              Then, I suppose,
when I was married, the use of Alistair's:
details forgotten or repressed.

In Dunedin I answered a small ad
and paid £10 for a museum piece
black and upright as a Model T Ford.

Next, a surprise: Barry Crump's portable
Empire Corona, an honourable
parting substitute for alimony.

It's rusting at the back of a cupboard
in case it should become collectable –
after all, he had his face on a stamp.

Then my Adler Gabriele: brand-new,
the machine 'für moderne Menschen' –
handsome and much cherished, until

the last one, a gift from my mother:
electronic with adjustable spacing
and a self-correct facility;

so efficient that for years I spurned
computers. Of them I shall say nothing.

Flat-warming Party, 1958

It's usual to have guests of both sexes;
but so far I don't know any women –
apart from my professor's wife, of course,
and I don't think it's her kind of party.

Therefore I have invited seven men,
including my self-proclaimed 'fiancé'
(not my title for him) who by the end,
with any luck, won't be speaking to me.

The Anaesthetist

He asked me 'Would you like to witness something?'
His signature on a document, I thought.
No; an emergency Caesarean.

He was my mother's friend – I hardly knew him;
but grist: yes, he saw I collected that.

The hospital was five minutes away;
he could pass me off as one of his students.
Gowned and masked, I sat in the gallery.

It took seconds: a slash down from the navel,
a transverse cut across the womb, and
they snatched a skinned rabbit out of a hat.

Then there was leisure to stuff wads of gauze
yard after yard into the seeping hollows,

to feather-stitch delicate inner tissues,
haul out the sodden scarlet dishcloths,
and cobble together white walls of fat.

'Wake up,' they said, 'wake up, Mrs Campbell' –
which happened to be my own name at the time.

Even so it was hard to identify
with her (this was like no birth I'd given);
easier, in a way, with the surgeon –

such a neat trick, once you'd been shown how.
If ever I were to find myself stranded
(desert island, snowbound cottage, stuck lift)

with a woman in desperate labour
and a handy scalpel I could have a go.

The Second Wedding

Photographs were by courtesy
of the *Otago Daily Times*:

'Author Weds Poetess' – a shot
of the bride wearing a dazed smile

in her new husband's Land Rover.
Her bruises don't show up at all.

(How easy it is to get cheap
effects with not a word untrue.)

This was after the registrar
had waited for us to put out

our cigarettes, and married us.
It was his job, and we were there.

The Sleeping-bag

But when we rolled him out he didn't move:
curled up like a bud. He'd fallen asleep
snuggled in the back of the Land Rover,

and Barry thought it would be amusing
to tote him up all those endless steps
to wherever we were visiting

like a sack of coal, over his shoulders,
swaddled in impermeable down.
Just hooliganism, really; a joke.

It may have taken seconds, not long minutes,
to shake him and shake him...
                    Light of my life
(child of my first marriage – nothing to Barry).

I have some friends who lost a son that way,
smothered in an airless den of feathers;
which, if I'd known... But not my son, praise God.

Barry could get away with most things.
Kids thought he was magic. They came flocking.
He was to kill five boys in his time:

by negligence, by booze, by his grievous fault.
They drowned, all five of them together, trapped
in a vehicle, unsupervised.

But my boy wasn't one of them.
(Let me not gloat, Lord. Let me not gloat.)
We'd moved on by then, I and my boy.

A Game of 500

The Muse is a seeker after sensation.
She wants me to tell you about the time
when my second husband offered to play me
at cards for my young lover's life.

Except that it wasn't quite like that:
no death on offer, for example; just
a beating-up. And anyway
he'd left me first, the bastard; and anyway...

But enough of that (although yes, I won).
What I'd rather tell you about is how
in this hot summer the little girls
have been chalking on the pavement:

birthday cakes with coloured candles,
and, repeated twice in large letters,
'Horse Queen of the Year' –
whatever they may have meant by that.

La Contessa Scalza

I'm at the bar on the swimming-pool deck,
chatting in German with Giuliano
and drinking Campari. My feet are bare
(hence my nickname) as if to symbolise
the shedding of a few identities –
or is it just a kind of showing off?
My five-year-old is in the cool playroom
two decks down, where the kids hoot and rollick.
Further down, in the hold, my worldly goods:
a large packing-case of household effects,
my sewing machine, Grandpa's cabin trunk
full of our clothes, two cardboard suitcases
splitting with books, and Barry Crump's cast-off
portable Smith Corona typewriter.

North London Polytechnic

Mr Yescombe explains my duties. One
will be to open what he calls 'the post'
(he means the mail). He introduces my
new colleague in the vast pink overall
who will show me around the library.

Then, making conversation, he assumes
I'll 'be wanting to visit Scotland soon'.
I simper politely. (No – why Scotland?
All I want is to wallow in the charms
of England regained after sixteen years.)

Meanwhile if I walk to the next-but-one
bus stop on the way home I'll save enough
to buy either the *Radio Times* (bliss
that it's not the *NZ Listener*) or
a loaf of bread. I'll decide which later.

Election, 1964

Mr Overton, the librarian
of the Commonwealth Relations Office,
came into Cataloguing to bring us
the election result: Labour had won.

'But don't worry,' he added, 'with such a
small majority I don't imagine
they'll be able to nationalise steel.'
I glanced at my colleague, a Sloane Ranger,

and at Mr Overton's kindly face.
These were the English, or samples of them.
How had I got through the vetting system?
This was hardly the moment to confess

it was I who had adorned the mirror
in the Ladies with 'Vote Labour' stickers.
Steel? What did I know about anything?
In New Zealand we had the Welfare State.

Kidnapped

That humming sound you can hear is of bees
feasting on the blossoming cherry tree
outside East Finchley Methodist Church,
into which my little boy was kidnapped
for a year or two of Sunday mornings
to march up and down the County roads
in his navy Boys' Brigade band jersey
and a round sailor-boy hat, yo-ho-ho,
playing whatever instrument he played
and not forgetting his penny for Jesus –
his reward being to appear onstage
at the Sunday school end-of-term gala
in the role of a chrysanthemum petal,
or a letter in the word 'chrysanthemum'.

II

Ann Jane's Husband

Consider for a moment Hugh Devlin,
sail-maker, of Liverpool,
who was married to Ann Jane Eggington
for six weeks before she died.

He must certainly have thought he'd killed her:
fucked her to death, most likely,
clutching her in his arms night after night,
his poor Ann Jane, and pumping

something unforgivable into her
until it erupted in
fever and screaming pain – his fault, surely.
No use to reason with him,

and he could conceivably have been right:
peritonitis can stem
from ectopic pregnancy. For the next
fifty years he bumped around

the dockside alleys, lodging with workmates,
his life lopped off at the root;
a non-ancestor. He would never risk
murdering a second wife.

Mother's Knee

I

If you like stories, here's one to chew on:
a little girl in the street at Cookstown
frightened by something she can't understand –
four men holding the corners of a sheet,
and tossing a body high in the air.

Hustling her away, her mother explained:
the one in the nightshirt had a fever;
that was the only way to bring it down.
Martha was five in 1848;
this must have been the Potato Famine.

II

A generation on, in New Zealand,
we come to Jinnie and the string of beads.
Her teenage sister Lizzie went swimming
at Slippery Creek with Phoebe Godkin,
and little Jinnie was left in their charge.

The only thing was to buy her silence.
Back home, Martha frightened it out of her:
'Where did you get those beads, Jinnie? Jinnie! '
'Phoebe Godkin gave me them, not to tell
about her and Lizzie going swimming.'

III

These are in the pure oral tradition –
mother to daughter to daughter's daughter –
no dates, no writing. It seems almost wrong
to supplement it from outside sources.
Lizzie, for example, married a man

who drove a brewer's dray and smelt of beer;
his last drink was a bottle of Lysol.
You surely can't like knowing that? Better
to leave her in 1880-something
prancing in Slippery Creek in her shift.

Camisoles

Then there was my mother's sister Dorrie
who stitched and trimmed a dozen camisoles
in pastel silk fabrics for her trousseau,
only to discover, as the wedding day loomed,
that the brassière had made them obsolete.

The March

The Baths Hall

Ellen Wilkinson, in the foam bath at Barnsley,
sees only the road – which, at the moment,
is all I can see myself, being uncertain
as to what exactly the women's foam bath was,

except that she had it all to herself
while two hundred aching men from Jarrow
wallowed and soothed their feet in the men's pool,
also specially heated for their arrival –

the road from Wakefield to Barnsley, that is:
nearly ten miles of it, and she walking in front
until they arrived at Barnsley Town Hall
for a meal of hot potato pie, and the Mayor proclaiming

'Everything that Barnsley can do for you will be done.'
But before too long Ellen's puny shoulders
emerge from the foam, anadyomene.
She may have been a legend; she was not a myth.

Ellen and the Bishops

A two-faced lot, in her experience.
Leicester and his wife were hospitable,
but he was low down in the hierarchy.
Jarrow, that 'saintly man', had blessed the march

as it set out but then had to recant
and call it 'undesirable'. He'd been
got at by Durham, who wrote to *The Times*
of 'revolutionary mob pressure'.

'When the class struggle comes to the surface,'
said Ellen, 'progress is a thin veneer.'
Just as well she wasn't there in person,
to contaminate Durham cathedral

and waken the misogynistic bones
of St Cuthbert behind the high altar
to a tantrum. A campaigning woman!
He might have kicked the lid right off his tomb.

The Mascot

Then there was the dog: a labrador, they thought,
or a mongrel, or, someone said, a terrier
(does that look like a terrier to you?)
But certainly a gift to the reporters.

Paddy, its name was, or Jarrow – a stray
that tagged on to the march; or it was called Peter
and belonged to a woman in Hebburn.
Once it nearly pulled Ellen off her feet.

Oh, they liked that, the journalists:
petite Miss Wilkinson, trying to keep up,
tittuping along on her little tootsies,
taking three steps to every stride of the men,

hanging on grimly to the mascot's leash
as they formed up to march into a town.
A labrador will do for the sculpture
posterity is going to erect.

You, Ellen

Heroine

I plucked you out of a group photograph
in our family album: you, composed,
standing in the centre front; my father,
pleased with himself, just behind you, his head,
like yours, tilted slightly back – a habit
learnt from being among taller people.

You chaired the first UNESCO conference
(this wasn't it); you were from Manchester,
you'd been a teacher, you'd served in the Blitz –
you couldn't have been more his cup of tea.
'That's the Minister of Education,'
Mother would boast. So where was it taken?

Three women and fifteen men, all in suits
apart from one ARP uniform
(is that a clue?) Birkbeck suggests itself,
or, more likely, the WEA.
There's no one alive to ask. OK, then:
I shall have to interrogate the dead.

*

But the dead are giving nothing away.
They refer me to books. I've read the books:
your books, the books of others, pro and con,
occasional condescending asides
in memoirs by your contemporaries –
all grist, but these are not what I'm after.

I want your personal correspondence
(destroyed by your over-loyal siblings);

I want all the notes and scribbles you burned,
the private diaries you never kept.
Yes, I suppose I could plod through Hansard.
It won't exactly answer my questions.

I want your voice; they advise me to go
to the British Library Sound Archive...
Meanwhile, the name of that conference? Ah:
the dead have spoken up; my late father
wrote home about it to my grandparents.
Not madly interesting, it turns out.

The Fiancé

They couldn't work out what you saw in this
'flabby length of pump water' (your aunt's words);
'arrogant; physically revolting'
said your friends; and – oh dear – 'always sniffing'.

You wouldn't have been the first young woman
to get carried away by the wrong chap.
But couldn't they see it was politics
you were in love with? It was the pure flame

of Marxism that soldered you to him –
even so briefly. Years later, after
his *annus* not-very-*mirabilis*
as Westminster's first Communist MP

something still flickered between you, until
you moved unforgivably far ahead;
by which time you had a PPS who
could intercept the hate mail he sent you.

The Division Bell Mystery

Well, you were no Dorothy L Sayers,
but a politician without a seat
needs an avocation that will grip her,
and this was yours in 1932.

Your plot wobbles, your favourite suspect,
sleek and columnar in her haute couture,
leaves us cold; your MP/sleuth is a drip,
and your police a disgrace to the force.

But look, who's this? A young Cockney member
(you in disguise) has joined the cast, to roam
the terraces of your former Eden,
denied to you since you lost Middlesbrough.

Let no one doubt: your true heroine was
the House itself – the sprawling, echoing,
towering Mother of Parliaments;
which in a few years would let you back in.

The Shelter Queen

'Safety, Sanitation and Sleep', meaning
bunk beds and chemical lavatories
for the nightly hordes on the tube platforms
or in air-raid shelters. Twice in your life

the public acknowledged you as a star:
first on the Jarrow march, then in the Blitz,
when having dodged or tired out your minders
you drove your own car wildly through London

(no headlights in the blackout) to offer
what comfort there might be to the bereaved
after the Heavy Rescue men had left,
at the cost of your own sleep and safety.

They were less keen when you had to enforce
fire-watching for women as well as men,
but you knew best; you'd been bombed out yourself.
Also there was that severed foot you'd seen.

Herbert Morrison

Not easy for some of us to warm to
a politician who was to become
Peter Mandelson's grandfather – although
a bit of human warmth was what he craved,

his wife having long ago switched hers off,
around the time she banned coal fires (the dust!)
Picture him, then, the Home Secretary,
spending week-nights during the Blitz in his

office basement but country weekends at
his assistant Miss Wilkinson's cottage,
snug by her hearth, one of them on each side,
working on the papers in their boxes;

or ('Caesar's wife' and all that; no scandal)
at some other fireside on his rota:
the Wilmots', Lady Rhondda's; the Frasers';
Lady Allen's – oh yes; Lady Allen...

The Hat

What was the 'incongruous' hat they heckled
when you rushed up, flustered, to the dispatch box?
Couldn't they see you hadn't long to live?
(Your fit of asthmatic coughing stilled them).

I find I have a hankering to view
a parade of your hats, your suits, your dresses:

the black velvet with the broad lace collar
for your 'little waif' act, the apple green

worn with your red hair – and shingled, what's more –
that shook up the House when you first took your seat
('Dress dull,' Nancy Astor advised); the fur coat
you tactfully (or hypocritically)

shed before speaking on a Union platform.
You'd have done better to wear it more often
and to be less valiant about your duties –
going out in all weathers, catching your death.

To Ellen, in the End

I've been procrastinating, edging back
from your pop-star exit – prescription drugs,
a scatter of pills on the floor; the doubts;
the did-she, didn't-she kernel of it.

Except that it wasn't from addiction;
it was asthma yet again, as always.
And it wasn't from love, surely? Not for
Morrison's chubby arms back around you?

His biographer writes baldly: 'Ellen
Wilkinson committed suicide', and
I want to hit him. It wasn't like that –
although it wasn't not like that either.

Perhaps all you longed for was a night's sleep.
There was an inquest: accidental death.
The gossips carry on (here's me, for one).
Your defenders protest. There's always more to say.

III

Hortus

Dreamiest dream for years, this enchanted
amble through cliff-top gardens enamelled
in greens my brain-cells have just invented.

Refusing to wake, my fingers fidget
for a mouse to click on Save and store it
among my Favourites, to revisit.

A Spinney

May Tree

Now that the trees are my family,
the hawthorn is my older sister:
prickly, but to be envied.

Who said she could dress up like that,
in the salty reek of may?
When will it be my turn for white froth?

Crab Apple

But the adults never understood it:
our co-conspirator at the wood's edge,
climbable, flowering or knobbly with dolls' fruit.

VJ Day came. Drunk with glory,
they chopped it to bits for their victory bonfire.
A streetful of kids howled in desolation.

Elm

Trust me to fall for something doomed! –
the tree in my school grounds I hid in daily,
higher than roof-height, when I was new.

It's gone where all the elm trees go.
I can feel its fissured bark; I can still mourn
the branch Jean Oliver snapped when she tried to be me.

Horse Chestnut

The squirrels want me to grow a forest.
They plant acorns in my lawn;
I haul them out by the stems, like minims.

They plant a conker. A green hand shoots up,
and lo, I've stabled it in a pot:
a fistful of sticky-buds for next spring.

Yew

Some bird shat out a seed in the alley.
I dug up a stalk of green feathers
and set it in a lighter place to grow.

Summer by summer it fattens and fluffs out –
slow, but wiser than me.
I'm going to let it live for a thousand years.

Fox-light

Waking out of sleep paralysis
with a back-from-the-brink gulp for breath
and a sudden aversion to bed, I leap
to my feet and hurl the window open.

There is the garden in black and white,
moon-stencilled with shadows; I think of
Erasmus Darwin and his lunar friends
trotting over their lit landscapes to meet.

This is fox-light: illumination
for foxes to go marauding by,
as in the days before they were urban,
and in the days before that; before towns.

Albatross

An albatross chick can weigh ten kilos:
heavier than either of its parents.
In the Albatross Centre they showed us
a saggy fake one in white towelling
to flummox us with its weight when we tried
lifting it. Think of that around your neck –
or even the lanky lattice of bones
it grows into. Imagine earning that.

# #

Walking is the secret of it: alone
or, famously, the three of you setting off
at sunset, Wordsworth laying out his plan
for your ballad and Dorothy noting it down;

walking, that is, and having read 'almost
everything – a library cormorant',
so that when you began there rushed into your brain
helter-skelter as you strode the Quantocks

Mr Philip Quarll on his South Sea island
who destroyed a bird 'as was certainly made for
Nature's Diversion' and the *Arabian Nights*
the merchantmen at the Bristol quays
your friend Cruikshank's dream of a spectre-ship
a menagerie of creatures out of Bartram's *Travels*
the parti-coloured snakes in the Azores
around Hawkins' becalmed ship not to mention
the Bounty mutineers on their rumour-haunted
voyaging Cook's crawling phosphorescence
the dancing fires whatever they were
or the ice-fields from northern latitudes
that could stand so easily for the polar South
lit by celestial phenomena
to wonder at and echoing with spirit voices

plus of course Shelvocke's *'disconsolate black albitross'*
as prescribed by Wordsworth at the beginning.

# #

'It ate the food it ne'er had eat' –
biscuit-worms given it by the mariners,
until you edited them out.

This was no spontaneous effusion,
say what they might, but the work of ardent months,

and long after Cottle came from Bristol
to discuss the printing it foamed through your head,
demanding to be tinkered with, modernised, glossed:

a nautical image from your trip to Malta
spliced in, some Chaucerian diction expunged...

You didn't need Mr Grouch and his Preface –
'The Poem of my Friend has indeed great defects' –
to keep you going back to fondle it.

# #

Flying-fish lay their eggs on floating debris;
hard to avoid slurping them up together.
'It ate the food it ne'er had eat':

toothbrush, golf ball, tampon applicator ...
What percentage of albatross chicks
have been found with plastic in their stomachs?

All.
        And what about trawl fisheries? Hooks?
No doubt websites can provide some statistics.

# #

But here comes your Old Navigator again,
beginning and beginning and beginning...

Cheveux de Lin

This newly scutched and hackled wisp of flax
rescued from the floor of the beetling mill
after the tourist guide's demonstration

matches exactly (in colour although
not quite in texture) the curl clipped from my
son Gregory's head at his first haircut

before his tender squiggles gave way to
thicker strands that darkened to brown, then black,
then, in his fifties, became smudged with grey.

My Erstwhile Fans

Gone are the days when I was all the rage
among the workers at a factory
in Timişoara – or so I was told

by the foreman; not me personally
but Romanian versions of my poems
(perhaps the credit lay with the translator).

Ceauşescu was shot. Poetry gave way
to Western movies and pornography.
I was a victim of the revolution.

The Bookshop

That bookshop where the Longleys and I,
drifting among the levels and chambers
of its peristaltic convolutions
on the last morning of the festival,

were lured in different directions, sucked
and digested in the dreamy caverns,
until we lost sight of each other and
they disappeared – or, as it seemed to them,

I disappeared – (backtrack as we might
there was no reuniting under that roof),
has now itself, apart from its online
phantom, vanished. As they do. As they do.

Maulden Church Meadow

As this is one of the destinations
for my ashes after I'm cremated
perhaps I could start with a trial run:
frizzle up one of my little fingers
while I'm walking here, and scatter it fresh
among the cowslips by the tadpole pond,
or lop one off among the lady's-smocks
on the bridle path as a snack for foxes.

I scoured the hedges around this field once
looking for their den. I could have waited:
what else would you call that excavation
in the north-east corner of my garden,
scooped under the roots of the pissard plum?

You can't really believe they eat children.

Oscar and Henry

If you must have a dog, have a golden retriever
and settle for the lumbering devotion
of one like Oscar, so hugely fixated
that, his master having failed to convey

the concept of 'temporary' or 'back in a month',
he fell into a canine depression
and developed eczema, which mustn't be scratched;
thus causing himself the humiliation

of having to walk around for weeks
with his head in a bucket, or at least stuck through
the base of a bucket, the sides framing
his face like Dog Toby's Punch and Judy frill.

But perhaps it's not a breed for the city
where the temptations can be so corrupting –
think of Henry, who at the faintest sniff
of freedom through a not quite latched front gate

is off towards the High Road, across the traffic lights,
and in at Budgens' automatic doors
to snaffle up another chocolate bar
from the impulse buys at the nearest checkout.

Real Estate

'If you sold this place,' says my neighbour, 'you
could buy a little flat.' A little flat!
One with no room for half my books, no stairs
to keep my knees in flexible order,

one in which on no morning would my eyes
open to next door's silver birch, self-sown
in the days of Marjorie and her cats,
or the house-high pear trees next door but one.

And what would such a deal bring me? Money.
Money with which I could try to buy back –
in vain, the market being what it is –
my garden full of snails and foliage,

my hundred-year-old Codling apple tree,
my self-propagating, sempiternal
primroses, my falling-down lilacs where
the goldfinches pose on their birdfeeders,

my much-repaired and always ailing roof,
my inconvenient, unheatable
indoor spaces, my Victorian bath
just long enough for me to lie down in.

The Lipstick

If I throw it into a bin,
this lipstick I bought by mistake
which wears the same metallic case
as my regular Pink Brandy

but is so shudderingly wrong
that when I use it on my lips
it makes my face look cyanosed,
it will finish up in landfill,

seeping and oozing, leaking fats
through its patiently corroding
armour, wailing invisibly
into the soil with its puce voice.

Hair

Then, fingering my hair, he asks
'What colour would you call it? Mauve?' –

and briefly I'm transformed into
some exotic flibbertigibbet

with rings on her toes, drinking Pernod
and dressed in an assemblage of wisps,

till I remember: he's colour-blind.
'No; just grey. But thank you for asking.'

Pacifiers

They clutch at their phones the way we used to reach for
a packet of Silk Cut: separation anxiety,
a blocky shape to fondle in your pocket.

I had a black cigarette holder, with sparkles,
and a carved ivory one from Singapore.
Smoke fizzed and sang under my breastbone.

                    Them and their apps.

Bender

I can do better than Uri Geller:
I can bend not just forks, and spoons, and knives,
but whole drawers of cutlery at once.

I can bend railings and fence-palings,
vertical stripes on wallpaper,
the spines of books in rows on a shelf,

and, if I rotate the pages,
through 90 degrees, lines of type.
I do it with my eyes, at a glance.

– But how bent are they? Curved like a horseshoe,
or rippled as in a distorting glass?
And will they stay bent when you have bent them?

– They are like the waves in a mermaid's hair:
kinked and cranked, not permanently marcelled.
A drench in the vasty deep will uncrimp them.

Kinky eyes are a perversion, surely,
but rectitude returns if I close
my left, my sinister orb – that frail jelly.

Hot Baths

These days when anxious friends confide in me
about their intimate medical problems
it's never that they're afraid they're pregnant
and the situation is complicated
by not being sure whether the father
was that guy from Christchurch at my party
or, two days afterwards, up at Nick's place,
when we all stayed the night sleeping on floors,
our brilliant but unstable student friend –
far too young; and the one from Christchurch, well...
plus they've proved that the old wives' remedy –
casseroling yourself in a boiling bath
while drinking gin – serves only to make you drunk,
and not happy-drunk; sickening, really.

Standedge

Let's hear it again for Marsden
with its sudden baking Yorkshire sunshine
and the vicarage-garden-party hat
I scavenged from a charity shop –
immortalised by a kind lady
who clicked us leaning against your car
(look, those are white York roses in the hedge!)

Oh, and the tunnel was open then,
your kind of thing as much as mine.
We joined a good-humoured queue for the boat;
I boasted to the tour guide
about my ancestor's nephew, a legger
(what could be more authentic? I ask you!),
and we chugged entranced into the darkening vaults.

Hic Iacet

'Keep it short and don't talk about yourself.'
But there will be no self to talk about
in that land of the obituary,
in that night of twenty-four hours,
lying on the stones without a stretcher,
weightless, evacuated, no one's dear.

IV

Pakiri

Take me to see the *oioi*,
which sounds like an Australian marsupial
but is in fact a flowering rush.

Something's eeling about under the lilies.
There are clumps of complicated knitting
constructed of interlocking thorns,

and willow, which can't be stopped from growing –
chopped and stacked for firewood,
the logs are still sprouting green.

Willow, green willow, green willow:
you ran all along the creeks of my youth,
promoting yourself regardless;

but this is an artificial pond;
the willow can stay on the perimeter
with the rest of the non-indigenous –

is that an aye-aye in the *oioi*?
No: no lemurs allowed, although
Rosa would love a bush-baby.

Paint me an aye-aye, Rosa,
and one for your other grandmother.
Don't forget we saw a huhu.

Helensville

Small-town New Zealand's doing its thing
of channelling the 1930s
with its Plunket Rooms and the adjoining
public toilets (unfortunately shut),
its grand Post Office (now superseded
by a PostShop), and the slightly less grand
historic original Grand Hotel,
in Railway Street (but the station's closed).

Then there's the art deco Regent Cinema,
now an antiques business – owned, it turns out
when we stop the car to take a picture,
by a man whose face is familiar
to our driver – didn't he go to school
with her brother, somewhere altogether else?

Ruakaka

(for Gillian Whitehead)

Oystercatchers have flaked out, storm-weary,
on the grass verges down by the beach.
Up here the builders will be back in the New Year;
there's a fridge in a bedroom, an electric jug
on the floor where the kitchen's going to be.

You've made soup and salad; we three have brought
cheese, wine, fruit. The cutlery's borrowed
from Joyce and Ian; this evening, in return,
we'll join them downstairs and you'll cook for us all.
Steamy sunshine's mopping the garden dry.

I'm spelling out what you already know,
for the sake of completing another entry
in our intermittent travelogue:
Newcastle, Ambleside, London, Sydney,
Auckland, the Otago Peninsula

(where I adopted your father's binoculars
and prowled the shoreline, laughing at my first
spoonbill – clearly designed by Walt Disney)
and Northumberland, redolent of Hotspur,
hero of our first collaboration.

After him came a parade of heroines,
from medieval queens to my great-aunt Alice,
to sing their way through their difficult lives.
How they haunted us! KM and Iris,
Elizabeth Percy in Alnwick castle,

and Eleanor; Eleanor. I still have
the green towel I bought in the market
for us to take turns with in that grotty
Paris hotel, when we were on our way
to meet Bill for our tour of Aquitaine.

Blue Stars

To qualify as a New Zealander
I'd have to turn against the agapanthus.
This wasn't mentioned at the passport office,
but my New Zealand nationality
is a part-time thing – a bit of nostalgia.
Genuine applicants don't need to be told.

They drive around in their cars, glaring
at parades of handsome blue stars on stalks
along even the remotest roadside verge,
more abundant than Wordsworth's daffodils.
'Can you believe the size of these roots?' they
pant in their gardens, with spade and mattock.

A country that has no indigenous
wild flowers except those growing on trees
must submit to being colonised again
if it wants ground level decoration.
Too late to complain that you didn't mean it;
that's what they used to say about rabbits.

Yes, yes: not your fault; we know that. The seeds
get carried far and wide by car tyres.
I sit in whoever's back seat cooing
at the floriferous, fluorescent
clusters of miniature sapphire trumpets
carried erect on their marching stems.

I never set eyes on one in my youth
until – when did I visit the Duggans?
But this is the age of garden escapes:
colourful incongruities flourish
incontinently wherever it's mild,
like parrots escaped from an aviary.

Most are accepted – nobody minds
the odd wallflower – but these are villains:
the blue rosette is the booby prize.
Oh, and there's a white variety too,
a luminous constellation of petals
in moon-colouring... All right; I'll shut up.

Thank you all for your hospitality.
I'll leave you battling against 'those aggies'
and travel home on my other passport
to – guess what statuesque, architectural,
strap-leaved plants grown years ago from seed
in pots on my outside window-sills?

Fowlds Park

Who does his duty is a question
Too complex to be solved by me;
But he, I venture the suggestion,
Does part of his who plants a tree.

JAMES RUSSELL LOWELL

Or, as the plaque at the entrance has it,
'to complex', with the second 'o' left out
and impossible to insert later,
stone being stone. But thank you, Sir George Fowlds,
for this thirty-acre bowl of greenery
combining sports ground and arboretum.

Here I brought first Ella and then Cait,
as each in turn grew old enough for it,
to identify from *Which New Zealand Bird?*
the kingfisher at his regular station
on the telephone wire; rosellas pasturing
on the grass next to the children's playground.

Everything here matters to someone:
the swings, the coin-in-the-slot barbecue
(when it works), the Rocky Nook Bowling Club,
the perimeter path for the dog walkers,
the elegant sky-high landmark silhouettes
of the gum trees beside Western Springs Road.

The bastards will get their hands on it – sure to;
they will come with their development schemes...
But in the meantime here is this ancient
great-great-granny pohutukawa
catching the sun at exactly the right time
for my deep memory to photograph it.

So before the Friends of Fowlds Park line up
with their diagrams and their aerial views
of which historic trees are for the chop –
Norfolk Island hibiscus, Phoenix palm,
Moreton Bay fig, Japanese cedar,
four tulip trees, four maple, one red oak,

and at least six varieties of natives –
let's pay tribute to the stonemason
focussing so hard on the tricky words
that he slipped up just once on a short one,
thus rendering the whole quotation
impossible for a pedant to forget.

Mercer

The squalid tea of Mercer is not strained.

A.R.D. FAIRBURN

Brilliant, Rex. And now that's out of the way
two more reflections on Mercer station,
neither including the refreshment room.

I travelled alone on the Limited
up from Wellington, when I was sixteen,
awake all night reading Faust in German.

Mercer was the last stop before Auckland
for express trains. Grandma bustled across
and shepherded me by bus to Drury.

Not that Drury hadn't its own station –
her father Richey Brooks, newly arrived
from County Derry, worked for the railways

while the tracks from Auckland were being laid
and stood at Drury to flag the first train
through to the new terminus at Mercer.

(I like to imagine him dressed up in
his old militia sergeant's uniform.)
1875, it was; late May.

Well, *Ave atque Vale*, Main Trunk Line:
you lasted a bare century, before
the tourist industry converted you

into a luxury cruise-line on rails;
the masses may travel by air or road
like us, who've parked somewhere anonymous

65

on State Highway 1 (is this still Mercer?)
to browse through some bric-à-brac in a shop.
Rejecting teapots, coins, a stuffed monkey,

I yield to half a dozen table knives
with bone-coloured handles, warm in the grip –
you know the ones – still in their tattered box.

Alfriston

It shouldn't be Alfriston at all;
it should be Drury. But Drury went agley,
went off, went bung, turned into shit creek.

No relatives there except underground
in the Presbyterian cemetery –
register kept for years by Uncle Wyc –

where a clump of toitoi, three metres high,
bursts up out of the cracked concrete
over his parents' monumental grave.

What a laugh he had, and the friendliest
false teeth of all the great-uncles!
(Uncle Jim, we thought, was the best looking.)

But now it's Alfriston, a grid of a place,
lines on a map, that we must go to
when we visit my nearest cousin:

Rose; little Rosie, red-haired rosebud,
a toddler when I was five, a basic
ingredient in essence-of-Drury –

Stop that! We're in Alfriston now,
with two more cousins, Shirley and Barbara
(Auntie Flo's girls), and Rose's husband.

The table's adorned for afternoon tea.
Perhaps I'd like a mini-quiche?
(Hang on – isn't that a bit modern?)

Cream cracker with a slice of tomato?
Date loaf? Another of Rose's scones?
And surely someone's knocked up a sponge.

Thames

Rather alternative these days, Thames:
haunted op-shops full of fancy crockery,
tottering canyons of old wardrobes,
a sense of goods for sale that aren't on show.
Hippies cruise by like extras in a film,
togged up in beards and unlikely knitwear.

Most things that happened here happened a while ago:
like the gold rush, with its hundred hotels;
like the locomotive industry
(watch out or you'll turn into a museum);
like staying with Auntie Lizzie and Alma
on our post-war back-from-England tour.

They gave us exotic fruits with real cream
and a crate of nasty American sodas
to make us feel at home in New Zealand.
'That's not fat, it's muscle,' said Auntie Lizzie
when we thwacked her on the bum, enjoying
a new great-aunt we could be cheeky with.

From Pollen Street Auckland to Pollen Street Thames
Alma had come in her middle-aged bridehood,
having married that pillar of rectitude
Mr Belcher of Ezywalkin Shoes.
(You wouldn't dare to wallop Mr Belcher;
we rather doubted if he had a bum.)

Nearly seventy years on, the former
Ezywalkin declines to reveal itself –
how to tell one handsome but faded
shop-front from another? Even this café
has a past. (Whoops! There goes a funeral:
a squad of bikers roaring behind a hearse.)

When we've finished our toasted sandwiches
it's time for the next touristic indulgence.
Andrew offers the bird hide, approached
by a boardwalk over a mangrove swamp:
not quite as long as he'd remembered
but joyously a-flutter with fantails.

By now the chief museum will be open
(and don't worry about that hooter;
it's a call for the Volunteer Fire Brigade –
to which no one seems to be responding).
I thank my clever son for the fantails.
'That's OK – any time,' says the modest.

Raglan

What do you do in Raglan when it's raining?
You sit outside the library, it seems,
under the stone portico, soaking up
the free wi-fi. Or you bring your guitar
and huddle among the harmonists, while
the raindrops dance off the Phoenix palms
all along the centre of Bow Street,
de-dah, de-dah. What else can they do?

If you're not a raindrop, you could hang out
at the Blacksand café, or the Shack; or
there's the museum, but when you've seen it
you've seen it – and you've certainly seen it
when you were at school, if you live here.
Or you could dive off the bridge. Be careful.

Miramar Revisited

(for Marilyn)

Right: we get off at the stop near Kauri Street,
but at the other end, not the old tram stop –
the airport perimeter encroached on that;
Caledonia Street is the bus route now.

Approaching it from the opposite direction
transfers our house to the wrong side of the road;
and it's gone topsy-turvy – where's the front verandah?
Why has the garage moved to the right-hand side?

We aren't so naive as to ask what happened
to the one our father built from packing cases
for his bargain vintage Model T Ford –
'We're off to see the Wizard...' (he knew he was it).

Better check up on the rest of our surroundings.
You think you've identified the old cake shop;
I'm after the newsagent's and the grocer's
where we used to be sent to do the messages.

Knox Church, purveyor of such wholesome pursuits
as table tennis and square dancing, has gone,
swept up like Dorothy's house out of Kansas,
and as for the milk-bar, that could be anywhere.

God knows, my brain's boggled enough already
puzzling out directions with the sun in the north.
Reason doesn't seem to prevail on a sense
lodged as deep as my pituitary gland.

But we're not lost. We've made our expedition.
Sunshine has Technicolored the flat streets;
this three-dimensional wind will be excised
from our memories in a week or two: you'll see.

Carterton

...Of which my experience is limited to
the wind-raked station, with Kathleen waiting
to clasp us against her fluffy pink jumper,
and five minutes in a car from there to here:

a former thirty-room hotel, twice burnt out,
so that most of the lower floor is a blank shell
and you have to walk up twenty-six splintery
stairs to the family end of the dining room

where Kathleen's son-in-law, a chimney sweep
in a good way of business, has said a blessing
over our meal (no alcohol, of course –
they're all JWs – but a laden table).

Thirty rooms are a lot, even with most of them
not yet reconstructed: more than enough to store
the entire contents of Kathleen's house, shipped over
from Australia after her husband died,

and still in its containers. Not limitless space,
but even while we've been sitting here eating
ham and potatoes, cauliflower and fish,
passing salads to each other, we've squeezed in

the crab-apple tree from the wood near Kathleen's house
just round the curve in Woodside Way from our own,
more trees, the timber yard where we trespassed,
and our back garden complete with our four ducks.

We've spooled in the track across the common
Kathleen and I used to walk over to school
with our little sisters (mine's here beside me),
rolled up a road or two and stuffed them in somehow,

and compressed a double-decker bus to fit.
There's still the school itself to be folded up,
including the playground and the air raid shelters
under the playground (we're working on those),

and the pub on the green, or at least its back door,
where if you had money you could buy a bag
of Smith's crisps – yes, the ones you've heard about
with a little twist of salt in dark blue paper.

Tinakori Road

A house-sized box of atmosphere, complete
with authentic fittings, repro wallpaper
and the creepy photograph of the dead baby:
the Katherine Mansfield Birthplace, my choice
for an outing in my granddaughter's car
on this drenched morning. OK, Julia? Cool.

Heading back we pass our own family shrine,
the house where your father spent his infancy:
not literally the birthplace – he and Andrew
were born in St Helen's hospital – but
the 'Gregory Campbell Learns-to-walk-and-talk,
rides-a-tricycle, falls-out-of-a-tree-place'.

In between that house, number 245,
and the Birthplace at the far end of the road,
there used to stand the 'Garden-Party' house:
number 75, an even grander
KM residence, background to her teens
and a cherished focus for Mansfield scholars.

I wasn't there when they demolished it
for the motorway, but Prof Gordon was –
eighty years old, fizzing like a rocket,
bouncing in front of the bulldozers, crushing
the impulse to snatch a souvenir plank
(what, after all, could he have done with it?)

The same fate befell her old school – my school:
not the charmless Lego that's replaced it
but the creaky wooden structure where I sat
in what was reputed to have been her classroom,
gazing into the distance, being her...
Well, that's it, Julia. If we had more time

we could drive to where you spent your own childhood –
and there she'd be again, preceding us
to Karori, to another of her homes
and her first school. Was it your first school too?
No, yours was Karori West. Still, pretty close.
A kind of phantom stalker, that KM.

High Rise

I spy with my long-seeing eye
a row of rooms in monochrome lighting.
On the largest window someone has scrawled
'P' and 'G' for 'Parking Gallery' –
a sketch of a sign; work in progress.

Behind me in P for pohutukawa,
at something more like street level,
the first tui cranks up the morning.
It is not morning. It is 4 a.m.

This building stands on legs that don't match.

Turn around again. Way below,
at street level minus four or five,
something red and enormous
is reversing into or out of its den;
its indicators ding out the news.

Down to the left, traffic lights are chanting
with a flash, flash and a flash, flash
that boring song you'll never get rid of.

Everything hums: hills, harbour,
hubbub-to-come. But it's not dawn yet.
Look in the sky and Brother, Brother:
twenty floors up, floating in darkness,
fluorescent blue letters mean 'Keep out of my hair'.

The Old Government Buildings

There it sprawls, embodying magnitude –
but also symmetry – not sure whether
to label itself 'buildings' or 'building'.

Dignity would demand the plural, but
'Largest wooden building in the southern
hemisphere' denotes it as singular.

Admittedly it doesn't look wooden:
it could be stone with a thick coat of paint
(decorators' beige, I regret to say) –

which indeed must have been the ambition
of the architect who designed it in
'Italianate, Neo-Renaissance' style.

Stone may look handsomely governmental
but earthquakes crumble it. This wood still stands.
What if certain portions of it are now,

following a safety-conscious update,
bogus – fake wood imitating fake stone
in fibreglass? I still seem to like it.

A couple of thousand times I passed it
on trams, on buses, in taxis or cars,
on foot, in or out of school uniform,

alone, in company, pushing a pram,
very occasionally on a bike,
scarcely glancing to confirm its presence,

before it began staring back at me.
Once, when it was half the age it is now
and still an anthill of civil servants,

I actually set foot inside it
to scan the education department
lists for my School Certificate results.

Now it's architectural royalty.
In front of it, in bronze, Peter Fraser,
clutching his hat, coat and briefcase, trots off

to a meeting, flawlessly brought to life
by my old mate Tony Stones, genius.
He modelled my head, one day in Oxford,

out on his lawn (well, clay gets everywhere).
No one has ever stared with such prolonged
scrutiny right up into my nostrils.

Lotus Land

This place is unreal, of course.

JAMES McNEISH

Walk along Willis Street or Lambton Quay
and you can buy cherries at roadside stalls,
shipped up from the South Island for Christmas,
from Marlborough or the Clutha Valley.

I buy them by the kilo and take them
to all and sundry. Cherries, yes, cherries.

*(Did I mention the sunshine? The short stroll
down- or uphill to wherever you want?)*

*

This is what they mean when they say *whanau* –
assorted cousins on the trampoline,
blondies and redheads, all Polynesian,
and a new little dark one to pass round.

Beth, aged 12, big sister *par excellence*,
picks up each baby in turn to snuggle.

*(She's my eldest great-granddaughter. I too
am received in this blessed company.)*

*

In Unity Books I spot James McNeish –
whenever you go there you meet someone –
beached up reluctantly in his eighties.
We ask each other the standard question.

Oh yes, he says, it's insane – I'm working
on three books at the same time. Publishers...

*(If it weren't for the wind, rich oligarchs
would surely gobble up this fair city.)*

*

I've brought my bearded son to midnight Mass,
to sing loud carols in the cathedral.

The Bishop of Wellington wears dreadlocks
under his mitre – rather confusing
when viewed from the rear. He fixes me with
an alarming smile: 'The body of Christ.'